PERPETUAL PEACE

The Library of Liberal Arts
OSKAR PIEST, FOUNDER

The Library of Liberal Arts

PERPETUAL PEACE

IMMANUEL KANT

Edited, with an introduction, by
LEWIS WHITE BECK
Professor of Philosophy, The University of Rochester

. . . .

The Library of Liberal Arts
published by

 THE **BOBBS-MERRILL** COMPANY, INC.
A SUBSIDIARY OF HOWARD W. SAMS & CO., INC.
Publishers • INDIANAPOLIS • NEW YORK

Immanuel Kant: 1724-1804

PERPETUAL PEACE was originally published in 1795

. . . .

CONTENTS

· · · · · · · · · · · · · · · · ·

INTRODUCTION

In 1795, Immanuel Kant published his tractate, *Perpetual Peace; a Philosophical Sketch* (*Zum ewigen Frieden. Ein philosophischer Entwurf*). He had enthusiastically adhered to the American cause in the Revolution against England; like many Germans he had welcomed the French Revolution and—unlike them—had remained faithful to its purposes even after the Reign of Terror. For his constancy to revolutionary principles he had come to be called a Jacobin—as unfriendly an epithet as "fellow traveler" is today—and he was under a royal prohibition from writing and teaching on religious subjects. To publish this work in the reign of Frederick William III was an act of courage.

But peace and plans for peace were in the air. Prussia had just made peace with the revolutionary government in France; a people's government had won a victory and the right to exist, not only against the *ancien régime* of France, but against the whole concert of warlike powers of Europe. Kant cannily chose this moment to issue his analysis of the causes of war and the conditions of peace. That it suited the interest of the time is shown by the fact that it was, within a year, translated into both French and English.

The tractate is drawn up in mock-heroic style, with its several sections corresponding to those of the treaties of his day. The witty proem prepares the reader for the hard but just indictment to be brought against the approved statecraft of the warring dynasties of Europe. Yet there is an elevated seriousness in it, befitting its high subject. Kant was a republican and a humanitarian, as deeply committed to a defense of the rights and interests of mankind as any French or American revolutionary. He saw war as the supreme obstacle to be overcome on the hard road toward securing these rights and interests. He was a realistic student of history and politics, and he knew the practical man's deafness to Utopian plans. But he was also the author of a system of moral philosophy which, he believed, provided a philosophical rationale for those practical procedures seen by prophets of peace from Dante to Saint-Pierre, from Rousseau to Wilson and to the authors of the Charter of the United Nations, to be the only ones that can possibly lead to permanent peace.

Perpetual Peace—unlike some of Kant's other works—can be best read just as it is printed: straight from beginning to end. He sets up Preliminary Articles prescribing what states, as they now exist, must do to have peace; then he formulates Definitive Articles of political philosophy, showing what must be the constitution of the states and what must be the structure of a league of nations under international law if peace is to be lasting. He next turns to a study of the conditions which make men and states warlike, and which, he believes, give hope that they will eventually renounce this barbarity. Then there is a demand, in an acute Secret Article, that the philosopher should be heard in times of peacemaking; and the rest of the essay is what he, as a philosopher, has to say about *Realpolitik,* the ethical criteria of political measures, and the moral obligation to seek and preserve peace.[1]

This is the order in which the essay should be first read. But the careful reader will discern a different logic in it. He will see that there are four lines or phases of argument which, in their own arrangement, make Kant's theses clearer

---

[1] One section from *The Metaphysics of Morals,* Part I, "Jurisprudence," published in 1797, continuing this part of the argument, is appended.

than they may be in the treaty-like organization of the text. I shall try to make these four parts clear under the following headings:

PHASE OF THE ARGUMENT	CHIEF PLACES IN TEXT
(1) Anthropological, concerning the place of war and peace in history, and man's natural tendency to peace	First Supplement
(2) Moral-philosophical, concerning the priority of the ethical over mere political considerations, and the ethical ideal of peace	Secret Article, First and Second Appendixes, and the selection from the "Jurisprudence"
(3) Moral-political, concerning the moral foundation of states capable of establishing permanent peace	The Definitive Articles and part of First Appendix
(4) Pragmatical or technical, concerning the ways and means of implementing this ideal in an imperfect world	The Preliminary Articles, and some parts of the Definitive Articles

Of course the rubrics are not quite so sharp and the pattern is not quite so simple; for the arguments, in part interdependent, are not presented in such isolation as this listing might suggest. But the references in the second column are to the chief discussions of the respective topics.

(1) *The anthropological study of war and peace.* Human nature, it is often said, is so depraved that peace is only a futile dream; all idealistic plans shatter on the rocks of unregenerate human nature. Kant, who seems never to have

had a sentimental or flattering thought about mankind, nevertheless does not draw this pessimistic inference from his study of the litany of evils which is history. Rather, he argues that it is nature herself (including, of course, human nature as understood by scientists and historians) which is the ultimate guarantor of peace.

Kant is impressed by the "natural" opposition of man to man, and by what he elsewhere [2] calls their "unsocial sociability," which brings them together and forces them to co-operate in the works of both peace and war. Kant is, of course, opposed to the glorifiers of war who have sometimes claimed him for their own; but he is simply being realistic in recognizing the way in which, in the past, conflict has laid down the conditions on which co-operation, first in small groups and eventually between states, becomes feasible and actual. Even a race of devils, granted only that they are intelligent, would find it possible and necessary to co-operate and establish civil society; and states governed by intelligent devils would themselves in time find it to their interest to form leagues and alliances, to make treaties and fulfill them. How much more is this true of man! Peace is an edifice at whose foundation there are past wars, in which issues decided by force and violence have become the material of laws, subsumed under and refined by compacts, constitutions, treaties, and alliances. Kant believes that this trend, whose dynamics are found in the "mechanism of human passions," can issue in perpetual alliances, the condition of lasting peace.

Not that, as he warns us, human beings are disinterested spectators or passive beneficiaries of an inevitable progress. Peace is a stern moral task, not a shore reached by simply riding on a historical wave. Why, then, this historical, anthropological disquisition with its optimistic conclusion, interrupting, as it seems to do, the political and moral admonitions of the treatise?

[2] In his *Idea of a Universal History,* translated in Hastie's *Kant's Principles of Politics* and in Friedrich's *The Philosophy of Kant.*

Here, as everywhere in Kant, there is a stubborn distrust of fanciful ideals not in contact with the facts of life. In his systematic works on ethics, he always tries to show that it is possible for some law to be obeyed, some ideal to be achieved, before he declares the law to be binding or the ideal valid. That is why, for instance, in the first *Critique* he argues for the possibility of freedom of the will before, in the second *Critique*, he argues for the practicability of the moral law. Similarly here. Here the same realistic compunction makes him try to show that, judged from the standpoint of fact, peace is not a chimerical ideal. If men by nature were so constituted that they must inevitably war among themselves through all time, then the only perpetual peace would be that of the great burial ground of humanity, and the moral law, "There ought not to be war," would be vain. But he attempts, in this historical and anthropological study, to show that, moral considerations aside, man and society are not so constituted; thus his right to discuss the *moral* problem is established.

(2) *The argument from moral philosophy.* Peace cannot be left entirely to blind nature, and it is too momentous to be entrusted solely to lawyers and politicians acting according to rules of thumb or books of statutes not continuously subjected to moral review. Statements of fact, such as those drawn from the historians' observations, imply no obligatory laws or judgments of value; nor is obligation created by the arbitrary fiat of a sovereign. An obligation is to be justified or "deduced" from principles of pure practical reason, from what Kant calls the "metaphysics of morals." Only the application of moral judgment requires detailed knowledge of men and affairs; the moral principles themselves cannot be extracted from empirical knowledge. Thus ethics, the "science" of the morally necessary, takes precedence over politics, the "art" of the empirically possible. The first question on a political act, therefore, ought not to be "Is it feasible?" but, "Is it right?"

Having shown that peace is not, because of human nature, an impossible ideal, Kant now argues that actions directed toward peace are right and obligatory. There are two premises for this. Neither of them is drawn from attempted answers to the obscure question of what will secure happiness among mankind as a whole; there is nothing utilitarian, in the optimistic manner of the eighteenth century, in Kant's argument. The first premise is the categorical imperative [3] which enjoins us always to act on a maxim of respect for human beings as ends in themselves. Kant says that in warmaking the ruler does not obey this principle, and instead of respecting the citizens as persons, he treats them as things to be used—and used up. The second premise is the juridical principle which underlies the dynamics of government, that men ought to, and as rational beings do, seek to extend the reign of law.

Together these lead to a formula by which the rightness or wrongness of particular political maxims can be judged: this is the *criterion of publicity*. Actions whose maxims cannot be publicly exposed without thwarting the purpose of the action itself are not responsive to the rights of others, and are therefore immoral. Actions are right if they can be fully effective only when their maxim is known to those touched by the action, for in these actions the person is treated as an end in himself. These are actions which the person affected could himself have willed. Their maxim is one which both the agent and patient can regard as a law they would willingly decree for themselves and their fellows. Where such actions are willed, the persons are equal, lawgiving members of a realm of ends.

[3] As explained in the *Grundlegung zur Metaphysik der Sitten*, Section II. See translations by Lewis White Beck, "Foundations of the Metaphysics of Morals" in *Critique of Practical Reason and Other Writings in Moral Philosophy*, Chicago: The University of Chicago Press, 1949; and Thomas K. Abbott, *Fundamental Principles of the Metaphysic of Morals*, New York: The Liberal Arts Press, 1949.

(3) *The moral-political argument.* The political analogue of the realm of ends is a republic. In a republic, all laws are self-imposed, and government is by the consent of the governed. Only here is there any a priori reason to expect that the rights and interests of men will be honored. Thus Kant sees the moral law and its political corollary, the criterion of publicity, as the key to the constitution and international law which may secure us the blessings of peace.

The three Definitive Articles are moral laws, translated into the language of law and politics. Only the second, the organization of a league of nations, requires special comment here. It should be noted that most of Article II is concerned with the alliance of sovereign states; but at the end Kant says that this will not secure permanent peace. What is needed is actually a "continuously growing state consisting of various nations," in default of which alliances must be established, though they are in constant peril of breaking down. But Kant admits here that there is not the will to establish world government, and elsewhere [4] he says that such a dominion would be administratively unworkable. Therefore the most that men can hope for is a gradual approach to a condition of peace—an ideal to be approached asymptotically.

(4) *The political implementation.* The way to begin is to begin. The first steps must be taken by imperfect, warlike, perhaps despotic, rulers of states whose chief glory is self-aggrandizement. They must be convinced that war is fatal to them, yet inevitable under their usual political practices. Kant believes that slight changes—they undoubtedly appeared slighter in the eighteenth than they do in the twentieth century; they are certainly slight in comparison with the world-shaking, epoch-making revolutions of the Definitive Articles—these slight changes, he says, can re-

[4] In *The Metaphysics of Morals,* I, "Jurisprudence," § 61.

verse this suicidal trend and lead to a climate of opinion in which peace will not be regarded by politicians as a cynical slogan, and as a sweet but empty dream by the citizens. A little of the good faith, intelligence, and common decency which make civil society possible will work a subtle revolution in the ways of diplomacy, and make it a tool of peace and not of war.

One point in these articles is worth special attention: Kant's "realism." Most interpreters of Kant show little awareness of this aspect of his ethics. The argument that, for instance, one ought not tell a lie even to save the life of an innocent person is often taken to be a characteristic and unavoidable feature of Kant's moral philosophy, and it is often thought that nothing can save it from what appears to be this *reductio ad absurdum*. But in some important, though not so well known, ethical writings there is full and clear insistence—which is present at least between the lines of the better-known works—upon the need and rightness of elbowroom for practical, realistic, common sense. A fortiori there is room for it in politics, even moral politics. Kant never forgets that politics is the art of the possible; he asks only that there be a more just estimate of what *is* possible. While not sanguine by nature, Kant is convinced that more is possible than is envisaged in the essentially hopeless political view that war is unending.

LEWIS WHITE BECK

SKETCH OF KANT'S LIFE AND WORK

Immanuel Kant was born in Königsberg, East Prussia, April 22, 1724. His family were among the Pietists, a Protestant sect somewhat like the Quakers and early Methodists. Pietism's deeply ethical orientation and singular lack of emphasis on theological dogmatism became a part of Kant's nature and a determining factor in his philosophy. After attending the University of Königsberg and serving as tutor in several aristocratic families, Kant became an instructor at the University. He held this position for fifteen years, lecturing and writing on metaphysics, logic, ethics, and the natural sciences. In the sciences he made significant but, at the time, little-recognized contributions, especially in physics, astronomy, geology, and meteorology.

In 1770 he was appointed Professor of Logic and Metaphysics at Königsberg, and in 1781 he published his most important work, the *Critique of Pure Reason.* This work opened up new fields of study and problems for him at an age when most men are ready to retire; but for Kant there followed a period of nearly twenty years of unremitting labor and unparalleled accomplishment. Merely a list of the most important writings shows this: *Prolegomena to Any Future Metaphysics* (1783); *Idea for a Universal History* (1784); *Fundamental Principles of the Metaphysics of Morals* (1785) ; *Metaphysical Foundations of Natural Science* (1786); second edition of *Critique of Pure Reason* (1787); *Critique of Practical Reason* (1787); *Critique of Judgment* (1790); *Religion within the Limits of Reason Alone* (1793); *Perpetual Peace* (1795); *Metaphysics of Ethics* (1797); *Anthropology from a Pragmatic Point of View* (1798). He died in Königsberg on February 12, 1804.

Kant's personality, or at least a caricature of it, is well known. Most people who know nothing else of Kant know that the housewives of Königsberg used to set their clocks by the regular afternoon walk he took, and that his life was said to pass like the most regular of regular verbs. But a truer picture of his personality—less pedantic, Prussian, and Puritanical—comes to us from the German writer Johann Gottfried Herder:

I have had the good fortune to know a philosopher. He was my teacher. In his prime he had the happy sprightliness of a youth; he continued to have it, I believe, even as a very old man. His broad forehead, built for thinking, was the seat of an imperturbable cheerfulness and joy. Speech, the richest in thought, flowed from his lips. Playfulness, wit, and humor were at his command. His lectures were the most entertaining talks. His mind, which examined Leibniz, Wolff, Baumgarten, Crusius, and Hume, and investigated the laws of nature of Newton, Kepler, and the physicists, comprehended equally the newest works of Rousseau . . . and the latest discoveries in science. He weighed them all, and always came back to the unbiased knowledge of nature and to the moral worth of man. The history of men and peoples, natural history and science, mathematics and observation, were the sources from which he enlivened his lectures and conversation. He was indifferent to nothing worth knowing. No cabal, no sect, no prejudice, no desire for fame could ever tempt him in the slightest away from broadening and illuminating the truth. He incited and gently forced others to think for themselves; despotism was foreign to his mind. This man, whom I name with the greatest gratitude and respect, was Immanuel Kant.

L. W. B.

BIBLIOGRAPHY

General Works on Kant

Körner, S. *Kant*. London, 1955.
Lindsay, A. D. *Kant*. London, 1934.
Paulsen, Friedrich. *Immanuel Kant, His Life and Doctrine*. Translated by J. E. Creighton and Albert Lefevre. New York, 1902.

Works on Kant's Theory of Peace

Armstrong, A. C. "Kant's Philosophy of Peace and War," *Journal of Philosophy*, 28 (1931), 197-204.

Bourke, John. "Kant's Doctrine of 'Perpetual Peace'," *Philosophy*, 17 (1942), 324-333.

Crawford, J. F. "Kant's Doctrine Concerning Perpetual Peace," in *Immanuel Kant: Papers Read on the Bicentenary of His Birth*, edited by E. L. Schaub. Chicago, 1926.

Fackenheim, Emil L. "Kant's Conception of History," *Kantstudien*, 48 (1957), 381-398.

Friedrich, C. J. "The Ideology of the United Nations Charter and the Philosophy of Kant," *Journal of Politics*, 9 (1947), 10-30.

————. *Inevitable Peace*. Cambridge, Mass., 1948. Contains Friedrich's translation of *Perpetual Peace*.

Hocking, William Ernest. "Immanuel Kant and the Policies of Nations," *Advocate of Peace*, 5 (1924), 414-424.

Paton, H. J. *In Defence of Reason*. London, 1951. See especially the essays "Justice Among Nations" and "Kant's Views on International Law."

Sacksteder, William. "Kant's Analysis of International Relations," *Journal of Philosophy*, 51 (1954), 848-855.

Schulz-Gaeverniz, Gerhart von. "Peace," in *Immanuel Kant, 1724-1924*, edited by E. C. Wilm. New Haven, 1925.

Shawcross, J. "Kant and the League of Nations," *Contemporary Review*, 155 (1939), 566-572.

Smith, Mary Campbell. "Introduction," in Kant, *Perpetual Peace*, translated and edited by Mary Campbell Smith. London, 1915.

NOTE ON THE TEXT

The present translation is a revision of the one I first published in my *Kant's Critique of Practical Reason and Other Writings in Moral Philosophy* (Chicago: The University of Chicago Press, 1949). The material omitted from the Chicago edition is included here, and this translation is complete.

It is based upon a careful collation of the German texts included in the Cassirer edition (*Kants Werke*, Vol. VI [Berlin, 1914]) and in the Prussian Academy edition (*Kants Gesammelte Schriften*, Vol. VIII [Berlin, 1912]). I have also made use of the work of generations of translators of Kant, especially the work of W. Hastie and Mary Campbell Smith.

Bracketed footnotes are mine.

L.W.B.

PERPETUAL PEACE

PERPETUAL PEACE

Whether this satirical inscription on a Dutch innkeeper's sign upon which a burial ground was painted had for its object mankind in general, or the rulers of states in particular, who are insatiable of war, or merely the philosophers who dream this sweet dream, it is not for us to decide. But one condition the author of this essay wishes to lay down. The practical politician assumes the attitude of looking down with great self-satisfaction on the political theorist as a pedant whose empty ideas in no way threaten the security of the state, inasmuch as the state must proceed on empirical principles; so the theorist is allowed to play his game without interference from the worldly-wise statesman. Such being his attitude, the practical politician —and this is the condition I make—should at least act consistently in the case of a conflict and not suspect some danger to the state in the political theorist's opinions which are ventured and publicly expressed without any ulterior purpose. By this *clausula salvatoria* the author desires formally and emphatically to deprecate herewith any malevolent interpretation which might be placed on his words.

SECTION I

CONTAINING THE PRELIMINARY ARTICLES FOR PERPETUAL PEACE AMONG STATES

1. *"No Treaty of Peace Shall Be Held Valid in Which There Is Tacitly Reserved Matter for a Future War"*

Otherwise a treaty would be only a truce, a suspension of hostilities but not peace, which means the end of all hostilities—so much so that even to attach the word "perpetual" to it is a dubious pleonasm. The causes for making future wars (which are perhaps unknown to the contracting parties) are without exception annihilated by the treaty of peace, even if they should be dug out of dusty documents by acute sleuthing. When one or both parties to a treaty of peace, being too exhausted to continue warring with each other, make a tacit reservation (*reservatio mentalis*) in regard to old claims to be elaborated only at some more favorable opportunity in the future, the treaty is made in bad faith, and we have an artifice worthy of the casuistry of a Jesuit. Considered by itself, it is beneath the dignity of a sovereign, just as the readiness to indulge in this kind of reasoning is unworthy of the dignity of his minister.

But if, in consequence of enlightened concepts of statecraft, the glory of the state is placed in its continual aggrandizement by whatever means, my conclusion will appear merely academic and pedantic.

2. "No Independent States, Large or Small, Shall Come under the Dominion of Another State by Inheritance, Exchange, Purchase, or Donation"

A state is not, like the ground which it occupies, a piece of property (*patrimonium*). It is a society of men whom no one else has any right to command or to dispose except the state itself. It is a trunk with its own roots. But to incorporate it into another state, like a graft, is to destroy its existence as a moral person, reducing it to a thing; such incorporation thus contradicts the idea of the original contract without which no right over a people can be conceived.[1]

[1] A hereditary kingdom is not a state which can be inherited by another state, but the right to govern it can be inherited by another physical person. The state thereby acquires a ruler, but he, as a ruler (i.e., as one already possessing another realm), does not acquire the state.

Everyone knows to what dangers Europe, the only part of the world where this manner of acquisition is known, has been brought, even down to the most recent times, by the presumption that states could espouse one another; it is in part a new kind of industry for gaining ascendancy by means of family alliances and without expenditure of forces, and in part a way of extending one's domain. Also the hiring-out of troops by one state to another, so that they can be used against an enemy not common to both, is to be counted under this principle;[2] for in this manner the subjects, as though they were things to be manipulated at pleasure, are used and also used up.

3. "Standing Armies (miles perpetuus) Shall in Time Be Totally Abolished"

For they incessantly menace other states by their readiness to appear at all times prepared for war; they incite them to compete with each other in the number of armed men, and there is no limit to this. For this reason, the cost of peace finally becomes more oppressive than that of a short war, and consequently a standing army is itself a cause of offensive war waged in order to relieve the state of this burden. Add to this that to pay men to kill or to be killed seems to entail using them as mere machines and tools in the hand of another (the state), and this is hardly compatible with the rights of mankind in our own person. But the periodic and voluntary military exercises of citizens who thereby secure themselves and their country against foreign aggression are entirely different.

The accumulation of treasure would have the same effect, for, of the three powers—the power of armies, of alliances, and of money—the third is perhaps the most depend-

[2] [This is an obvious reference to the hiring-out of the Hessians to England in the American Revolutionary War only a few years before this treatise was written.]

able weapon.[3] Such accumulation of treasure is regarded by other states as a threat of war, and if it were not for the difficulties in learning the amount, it would force the other state to make an early attack.

4. *"National Debts Shall Not Be Contracted with a View to the External Friction of States"*

This expedient of seeking aid within or without the state is above suspicion when the purpose is domestic economy (e.g., the improvement of roads, new settlements, establishment of stores against unfruitful years, etc.). But as an opposing machine in the antagonism of powers, a credit system which grows beyond sight and which is yet a safe debt for the present requirements—because all the creditors do not require payment at one time—constitutes a dangerous money power. This ingenious invention of a commercial people [England] in this century is dangerous because it is a war treasure which exceeds the treasures of all other states; it cannot be exhausted except by default of taxes (which is inevitable), though it can be long delayed by the stimulus to trade which occurs through the reaction of credit on industry and commerce. This facility in making war, together with the inclination to do so on the part of rulers—an inclination which seems inborn in human nature—is thus a great hindrance to perpetual peace. Therefore, to forbid this credit system must be a preliminary article of perpetual peace all the more because it must eventually entangle many innocent states in the inevitable bankruptcy and openly harm them. They are therefore justified in allying themselves against such a state and its measures.

[3] [This is probably a reference to the mercantilistic policy of Frederick William I, who collected a state treasure which in turn gave Frederick the Great the means to wage the Seven Years War.]

No. 5. *"No State Shall by Force Interfere with the Constitution or Government of Another State"*

For what is there to authorize it to do so? The offense, perhaps, which a state gives to the subjects of another state? Rather the example of the evil into which a state has fallen because of its lawlessness should serve as a warning. Moreover, the bad example which one free person affords another as a *scandalum acceptum* is not an infringement of his rights. But it would be quite different if a state, by internal rebellion, should fall into two parts, each of which pretended to be a separate state making claim to the whole. To lend assistance to one of these cannot be considered an interference in the constitution of the other state (for it is then in a state of anarchy). But so long as the internal dissension has not come to this critical point, such interference by foreign powers would infringe on the rights of an independent people struggling with its internal disease; hence it would itself be an offense and would render the autonomy of all states insecure.

6. *"No State Shall, during War, Permit Such Acts of Hostility Which Would Make Mutual Confidence in the Subsequent Peace Impossible: Such Are the Employment of Assassins* (percussores), *Poisoners* (venefici), *Breach of Capitulation, and Incitement to Treason* (perduellio) *in the Opposing State"*

These are dishonorable stratagems. For some confidence in the character of the enemy must remain even in the midst of war, as otherwise no peace could be concluded and the hostilities would degenerate into a war of extermination (*bellum internecinum*). War, however, is only the sad recourse in the state of nature (where there is no tribunal which could judge with the force of law) by which each state asserts its right by violence and in which neither party can be adjudged unjust (for that would presuppose a juridical decision); in lieu of such a decision, the issue of the conflict (as if given by a so-called "judgment of God") decides on which side justice lies. But between states no punitive war (*bellum punitivum*) is conceivable, because there is no relation between them of master and servant.

It follows that a war of extermination, in which the destruction of both parties and of all justice can result, would permit perpetual peace only in the vast burial ground of the human race. Therefore, such a war and the use of all means leading to it must be absolutely forbidden. But that the means cited do inevitably lead to it is clear from the fact that these infernal arts, vile in themselves, when once used would not long be confined to the sphere of war. Take, for instance, the use of spies (*uti exploratoribus*). In this, one employs the infamy of others (which can never be entirely eradicated) only to encourage its persistence even into the state of peace, to the undoing of the very spirit of peace.

Although the laws stated are objectively, i.e., in so far as they express the intention of rulers, mere prohibitions (*leges prohibitivae*), some of them are of that strict kind which hold regardless of circumstances (*leges strictae*) and which demand prompt execution. Such are Nos. 1, 5, and 6. Others, like Nos. 2, 3, and 4, while not exceptions from the rule of law, nevertheless are subjectively broader (*leges latae*) in respect to their observation, containing permission to delay their execution without, however, losing sight of the end. This permission does not authorize, under No. 2, for example, delaying until doomsday (or, as Augustus used to say, *ad calendas Graecas*) the re-establishment of the freedom of states which have been deprived of it—i.e., it does not permit us to fail to do it, but it allows a delay to prevent precipitation which might injure the goal striven for. For the prohibition concerns only the manner of acquisition which is no longer permitted, but not the possession, which, though not bearing a requisite title of right, has nevertheless been held lawful in all states by the public opinion of the time (the time of the putative acquisition).[4]

[4] It has not without cause hitherto been doubted whether besides the commands (*leges praeceptivae*) and prohibitions (*leges prohibitivae*) there could also be permissive laws (*leges permissivae*) of pure reason. For laws as such contain a principle of objective practical necessity, while permission implies a principle of the practical contingency of certain actions. Hence a law of permission would imply constraint to an action to do that to which no one can be constrained. If the object of the law has the same meaning in both cases, this is a contradiction. But in permissive law, which is in question here, the prohibition refers only to the future mode of acquisition of a right (e.g., by succession), while the permission annuls this prohibition only with reference to the present possession. This possession, though only putative, may be held to be just (*possessio putativa*) in the transition from the state of nature to a civil state, by virtue of a permissive law included under natural law, even though it is [strictly] illegal. But, as soon as it is recognized as illegal in the state of nature, a similar mode of acquisition in the subsequent civil state (after this transition has occurred) is forbidden, and this right to continuing possession would not hold if such a presumptive acquisition had taken place in the civil state. For in this case it would be an infringement which would have to cease as soon as its illegality was discovered.

I have wished only to call the attention of the teachers of natural law to the concept of a *lex permissiva*, which systematic reason affords, particularly since in civil (statute) law use is often made of it. But in the ordinary use of it, there is this difference: prohibitive law stands alone, while permission is not introduced into it as a limiting condition (as it should be) but counted among the exceptions to it. Then it is said, "This or that is forbidden, except Nos. 1, 2, 3," and so on indefinitely. These exceptions are added to the law only as an afterthought required by our groping around among cases as they arise, and not by any principle. Otherwise the conditions would have had to be introduced into the formula of the prohibition, and in this way it would itself have become a permissive law. It is, therefore, unfortunate that the subtle question proposed by the wise and acute Count von Windischgrätz * was never answered and soon consigned to oblivion, because it insisted on the point here discussed. For the possibility

* [Reichsgraf Josef Niklas von Windischgrätz (1744-1802) proposed the following question for a prize essay: "How can contracts be drawn which will be susceptible to no divergent interpretation, and by which any suit concerning transfer of property will be impossible, so that no legal process can arise from any document having this proposed form?"]

SECTION II

CONTAINING THE DEFINITIVE ARTICLES FOR PERPETUAL PEACE AMONG STATES

The state of peace among men living side by side is not the natural state (*status naturalis*); the natural state is one of war. This does not always mean open hostilities, but at least an unceasing threat of war. A state of peace, therefore, must be *established,* for in order to be secured against hostility it is not sufficient that hostilities simply be not committed; and, unless this security is pledged to each by his neighbor (a thing that can occur only in a civil state), each may treat his neighbor, from whom he demands this security, as an enemy.[1]

---

of a formula similar to those of mathematics is the only legitimate criterion of a consistent legislation, and without it the so-called *ius certum* must always remain a pious wish. Otherwise we shall have merely general laws (which apply to a great number of cases), but no universal laws (which apply to all cases) as the concept of a law seems to require.

[1] We ordinarily assume that no one may act inimically toward another except when he has been actively injured by the other. This is quite correct if both are under civil law, for, by entering into such a state, they afford each other the requisite security through the sovereign which has power over both. Man (or the people) in the state of nature deprives me of this security and injures me, if he is near me, by this mere status of his, even though he does not injure me actively (*facto*); he does so by the lawlessness of his condition (*statu iniusto*) which constantly threatens me. Therefore, I can compel him either to enter with me into a state of civil law or to remove himself from my neighborhood. The postulate which is basic to all the following articles is: All men who can reciprocally influence each other must stand under some civil constitution.

Every juridical constitution which concerns the person who stands under it is one of the following:

(1) The constitution conforming to the civil law of men in a nation (*ius civitatis*).

FIRST DEFINITIVE ARTICLE FOR PERPETUAL PEACE

"*The Civil Constitution of Every State Should Be Republican*"

The only constitution which derives from the idea of the original compact, and on which all juridical legislation of a people must be based, is the republican.[2] This constitu-

(2) The constitution conforming to the law of nations in their relation to one another (*ius gentium*).

(3) The constitution conforming to the law of world citizenship, so far as men and states are considered as citizens of a universal state of men, in their external mutual relationships (*ius cosmopoliticum*).

This division is not arbitrary, being necessary in relation to the idea of perpetual peace. For if only one state were related to another by physical influence and were yet in a state of nature, war would necessarily follow, and our purpose here is precisely to free ourselves of war.

[2] Juridical (and hence) external freedom cannot be defined, as is usual, by the privilege of doing anything one wills so long as he does not injure another. For what is a privilege? It is the possibility of an action so far as one does not injure anyone by it. Then the definition would read: Freedom is the possibility of those actions by which one does no one an injury. One does another no injury (he may do as he pleases) only if he does another no injury—an empty tautology. Rather, my external (juridical) freedom is to be defined as follows: It is the privilege to lend obedience to no external laws except those to which I could have given consent. Similarly, external (juridical) equality in a state is that relationship among the citizens in which no one can lawfully bind another without at the same time subjecting himself to the law by which he also can be bound. No definition of juridical dependence is needed, as this already lies in the concept of a state's constitution as such.

The validity of these inborn rights, which are inalienable and belong necessarily to humanity, is raised to an even higher level by the principle of the juridical relation of man to higher beings, for, if he believes in them, he regards himself by the same principles as a citizen of a supersensuous world. For in what concerns my freedom, I have no obligation with respect to divine law, which can be acknowledged by my reason alone, except in so far as I could have given my consent to it. Indeed, it is only through the law of freedom of my own reason that I frame a concept of the divine will. With regard to

tion is established, firstly, by principles of the freedom of the members of a society (as men); secondly, by principles of dependence of all upon a single common legislation (as subjects); and, thirdly, by the law of their equality (as citizens). The republican constitution, therefore, is, with respect to law, the one which is the original basis of every form of civil constitution. The only question now is: Is it also the one which can lead to perpetual peace?

The republican constitution, besides the purity of its origin (having sprung from the pure source of the concept of law), also gives a favorable prospect for the desired consequence, i.e., perpetual peace. The reason is this: if the consent of the citizens is required in order to decide that war should be declared (and in this constitution it cannot but be the case), nothing is more natural than that they would be very cautious in commencing such a poor game,

---

the most sublime reason in the world that I can think of, with the exception of God—say, the great Aeon—when I do my duty in my post as he does in his, there is no reason under the law of equality why obedience to duty should fall only to me and the right to command only to him. The reason why this principle of equality does not pertain to our relation to God (as the principle of freedom does) is that this Being is the only one to which the concept of duty does not apply.

But with respect to the right of equality of all citizens as subjects, the question of whether a hereditary nobility may be tolerated turns upon the answer to the question as to whether the pre-eminent rank granted by the state to one citizen over another ought to precede merit or follow it. Now it is obvious that, if rank is associated with birth, it is uncertain whether merit (political skill and integrity) will also follow; hence it would be as if a favorite without any merit were given command. The general will of the people would never agree to this in the original contract, which is the principle of all law, for a nobleman is not necessarily a noble man. With regard to the nobility of office (as we might call the rank of the higher magistracy) which one must earn by merit, this rank does not belong to the person as his property; it belongs to his post, and equality is not thereby infringed, because when a man quits his office he renounces the rank it confers and re-enters into the class of his fellows.

decreeing for themselves all the calamities of war. Among the latter would be: having to fight, having to pay the costs of war from their own resources, having painfully to repair the devastation war leaves behind, and, to fill up the measure of evils, load themselves with a heavy national debt that would embitter peace itself and that can never be liquidated on account of constant wars in the future. But, on the other hand, in a constitution which is not republican, and under which the subjects are not citizens, a declaration of war is the easiest thing in the world to decide upon, because war does not require of the ruler, who is the proprietor and not a member of the state, the least sacrifice of the pleasures of his table, the chase, his country houses, his court functions, and the like. He may, therefore, resolve on war as on a pleasure party for the most trivial reasons, and with perfect indifference leave the justification which decency requires to the diplomatic corps who are ever ready to provide it.

In order not to confuse the republican constitution with the democratic (as is commonly done), the following should be noted. The forms of a state (*civitas*) can be divided either according to the persons who possess the sovereign power or according to the mode of administration exercised over the people by the chief, whoever he may be. The first is properly called the form of sovereignty (*forma imperii*), and there are only three possible forms of it: autocracy, in which one, aristocracy, in which some associated together, or democracy, in which all those who constitute society, possess sovereign power. They may be characterized, respectively, as the power of a monarch, of the nobility, or of the people. The second division is that by the form of government (*forma regiminis*) and is based on the way in which the state makes use of its power; this way is based on the constitution, which is the act of the general will through which the many persons become one nation.

In this respect government is either republican or despotic. Republicanism is the political principle of the separation of the executive power (the administration) from the legislative; despotism is that of the autonomous execution by the state of laws which it has itself decreed. Thus in a despotism the public will is administered by the ruler as his own will. Of the three forms of the state, that of democracy is, properly speaking, necessarily a despotism, because it establishes an executive power in which "all" decide for or even against one who does not agree; that is, "all," who are not quite all, decide, and this is a contradiction of the general will with itself and with freedom.

Every form of government which is not representative is, properly speaking, without form. The legislator can unite in one and the same person his function as legislative and as executor of his will just as little as the universal of the major premise in a syllogism can also be the subsumption of the particular under the universal in the minor. And even though the other two constitutions are always defective to the extent that they do leave room for this mode of administration, it is at least possible for them to assume a mode of government conforming to the spirit of a representative system (as when Frederick II [3] at least *said* he was merely the first servant of the state).[4] On the other hand, the democratic mode of government makes this impossible, since everyone wishes to be master. Therefore, we can say:

3 [Frederick the Great, in his *Anti-Macchiavel*.]

4 The lofty epithets of "the Lord's anointed," "the executor of the divine will on earth," and "the vicar of God," which have been lavished on sovereigns, have been frequently censured as crude and intoxicating flatteries. But this seems to me without good reason. Far from inspiring a monarch with pride, they should rather render him humble, providing he possesses some intelligence (which we must assume). They should make him reflect that he has taken an office too great for man, an office which is the holiest God has ordained on earth, to be the trustee of the rights of men, and that he must always stand in dread of having in some way injured this "apple of God's eye."

the smaller the personnel of the government (the smaller the number of rulers), the greater is their representation and the more nearly the constitution approaches to the possibility of republicanism; thus the constitution may be expected by gradual reform finally to raise itself to republicanism. For these reasons it is more difficult for an aristocracy than for a monarchy to achieve the one completely juridical constitution, and it is impossible for a democracy to do so except by violent revolution.

The mode of government,[5] however, is incomparably more important to the people than the form of sovereignty, although much depends on the greater or lesser suitability of the latter to the end of [good] government. To conform to the concept of law, however, government must have a representative form, and in this system only a republican mode of government is possible; without it, government is despotic and arbitrary, whatever the constitution may be. None of the ancient so-called "republics" knew this system, and they all finally and inevitably degenerated into despotism under the sovereignty of one, which is the most bearable of all forms of despotism.

[5] Mallet du Pan,* in his pompous but empty and hollow language, pretends to have become convinced, after long experience, of the truth of Pope's well-known saying:

"For forms of government let fools contest:
Whate'er is best administered, is best." †

If that means that the best-administered state is the state that is best administered, he has, to make use of Swift's expression, "cracked a nut to come at a maggot." But if it means that the best-administered state also has the best mode of government, i.e., the best constitution, then it is thoroughly wrong, for examples of good governments prove nothing about the form of government. Whoever reigned better than a Titus and a Marcus Aurelius? Yet one was succeeded by a Domitian and the other by a Commodus. This could never have happened under a good constitution, for their unworthiness for this post was known early enough and also the power of the ruler was sufficient to have excluded them.

* [Jacques Mallet du Pan (1749-1800), in his *Über die französische Revolution und die Ursachen ihrer Dauer* (1794).]
† [*Essay on Man*, III, 303-4.]

SECOND DEFINITIVE ARTICLE FOR A PERPETUAL PEACE

"The Law of Nations Shall be Founded on a Federation of Free States"

Peoples, as states, like individuals, may be judged to injure one another merely by their coexistence in the state of nature (i.e., while independent of external laws). Each of them may and should for the sake of its own security demand that the others enter with it into a constitution similar to the civil constitution, for under such a constitution each can be secure in his right. This would be a league of nations, but it would not have to be a state consisting of nations. That would be contradictory, since a state implies the relation of a superior (legislating) to an inferior (obeying), i.e., the people, and many nations in one state would then constitute only one nation. This contradicts the presupposition, for here we have to weigh the rights of nations against each other so far as they are distinct states and not amalgamated into one.

When we see the attachment of savages to their lawless freedom, preferring ceaseless combat to subjection to a lawful constraint which they might establish, and thus preferring senseless freedom to rational freedom, we regard it with deep contempt as barbarity, rudeness, and a brutish degradation of humanity. Accordingly, one would think that civilized people (each united in a state) would hasten all the more to escape, the sooner the better, from such a depraved condition. But, instead, each state places its majesty (for it is absurd to speak of the majesty of the people) in being subject to no external juridical restraint, and the splendor of its sovereign consists in the fact that many thousands stand at his command to sacrifice themselves for something that does not concern them and without his needing to place himself in the least danger.[6] The chief

---

[6] A Bulgarian prince gave the following answer to the Greek emperor who good-naturedly suggested that they settle their difference

is not to be lost, there can be, then, in place of the positive idea of a world republic, only the negative surrogate of an alliance which averts war, endures, spreads, and holds back the stream of those hostile passions which fear the law, though such an alliance is in constant peril of their breaking loose again.[8] *Furor impius intus . . . fremit horridus ore cruento* (Virgil).[9]

THIRD DEFINITIVE ARTICLE FOR A PERPETUAL PEACE

"The Law of World Citizenship Shall Be Limited to Conditions of Universal Hospitality"

Here, as in the preceding articles, it is not a question of philanthropy but of right. Hospitality means the right of a stranger not to be treated as an enemy when he arrives in the land of another. One may refuse to receive him when this can be done without causing his destruction; but, so long as he peacefully occupies his place, one may not treat him with hostility. It is not the right to be a permanent

[8] It would not ill become a people that has just terminated a war to decree, besides a day of thanksgiving, a day of fasting in order to ask heaven, in the name of the state, for forgiveness for the great iniquity which the human race still goes on to perpetuate in refusing to submit to a lawful constitution in their relation to other peoples, preferring, from pride in their independence, to make use of the barbarous means of war even though they are not able to attain what is sought, namely, the rights of a single state. The thanksgiving for victory won during the war, the hymns which are sung to the God of Hosts (in good Israelitic manner), stand in equally sharp contrast to the moral idea of the Father of Men. For they not only show a sad enough indifference to the way in which nations seek their rights, but in addition express a joy in having annihilated a multitude of men or their happiness.

[9] ["Within, impious Rage, sitting on savage arms, his hands fast bound behind with a hundred brazen knots, shall roar in the ghastliness of blood-stained lips" (*Aeneid* I, 294-96, trans. H. Rushton Fairclough, "Loeb Classical Library," Cambridge: Harvard University Press, 1926).]

difference between European and American savages lies in the fact that many tribes of the latter have been eaten by their enemies, while the former know how to make better use of their conquered enemies than to dine off them; they know better how to use them to increase the number of their subjects and thus the quantity of instruments for even more extensive wars.

When we consider the perverseness of human nature which is nakedly revealed in the uncontrolled relations between nations (this perverseness being veiled in the state of civil law by the constraint exercised by government), we may well be astonished that the word "law" has not yet been banished from war politics as pedantic, and that no state has yet been bold enough to advocate this point of view. Up to the present, Hugo Grotius, Pufendorf, Vattel,[7] and many other irritating comforters have been cited in justification of war, though their code, philosophically or diplomatically formulated, has not and cannot have the least legal force, because states as such do not stand under a common external power. There is no instance on record that a state has ever been moved to desist from its purpose because of arguments backed up by the testimony of such great men. But the homage which each state pays (at least in words) to the concept of law proves that there is slumbering in man an even greater moral disposition to become master of the evil principle in himself (which he cannot disclaim) and to hope for the same from others. Otherwise the word "law" would never be pronounced by states which wish to war upon one another; it would be used only ironically, as a Gallic prince interpreted it when he said, "It is

by a duel: "A smith who has tongs won't pluck the glowing iron from the fire with his bare hands."

[7] [Hugo Grotius (1583-1645), Samuel von Pufendorf (1632-1694), and Emer de Vattel (1714-1767) developed systems of international law which recognized the legitimacy of some wars. See Grotius, *De jure belli ac pacis* (1625), Pufendorf, *De jure naturae et gentium* (1672), Vattel, *Le Droit des gens* (1758).]

the prerogative which nature has given the stronger that the weaker should obey him."

States do not plead their cause before a tribunal; war alone is their way of bringing suit. But by war and its favorable issue in victory, right is not decided, and though by a treaty of peace this particular war is brought to an end, the state of war, of always finding a new pretext to hostilities, is not terminated. Nor can this be declared wrong, considering the fact that in this state each is the judge of his own case. Notwithstanding, the obligation which men in a lawless condition have under the natural law, and which requires them to abandon the state of nature, does not quite apply to states under the law of nations, for as states they already have an internal juridical constitution and have thus outgrown compulsion from others to submit to a more extended lawful constitution according to their ideas of right. This is true in spite of the fact that reason, from its throne of supreme moral legislating authority, absolutely condemns war as a legal recourse and makes a state of peace a direct duty, even though peace cannot be established or secured except by a compact among nations.

For these reasons there must be a league of a particular kind, which can be called a league of peace (*foedus pacificum*), and which would be distinguished from a treaty of peace (*pactum pacis*) by the fact that the latter terminates only one war, while the former seeks to make an end of all wars forever. This league does not tend to any dominion over the power of the state but only to the maintenance and security of the freedom of the state itself and of other states in league with it, without there being any need for them to submit to civil laws and their compulsion, as men in a state of nature must submit.

The practicability (objective reality) of this idea of federation, which should gradually spread to all states and thus lead to perpetual peace, can be proved. For if fortune directs that a powerful and enlightened people can make

itself a republic, which by its nature must be inclined to perpetual peace, this gives a fulcrum to the federation with other states so that they may adhere to it and thus secure freedom under the idea of the law of nations. By more and more such associations, the federation may be gradually extended.

We may readily conceive that a people should say, "There ought to be no war among us, for we want to make ourselves into a state; that is, we want to establish a supreme legislative, executive, and judiciary power which will reconcile our differences peaceably." But when this state says, "There ought to be no war between myself and other states, even though I acknowledge no supreme legislative power by which our rights are mutually guaranteed," it is not at all clear on what I can base my confidence in my own rights unless it is the free federation, the surrogate of the civil social order, which reason necessarily associates with the concept of the law of nations—assuming that something is really meant by the latter.

The concept of a law of nations as a right to make war does not really mean anything, because it is then a law of deciding what is right by unilateral maxims through force and not by universally valid public laws which restrict the freedom of each one. The only conceivable meaning of such a law of nations might be that it serves men right who are so inclined that they should destroy each other and thus find perpetual peace in the vast grave that swallows both the atrocities and their perpetrators. For states in their relation to each other, there cannot be any reasonable way out of the lawless condition which entails only war except that they, like individual men, should give up their savage (lawless) freedom, adjust themselves to the constraints of public law, and thus establish a continuously growing state consisting of various nations (*civitas gentium*), which will ultimately include all the nations of the world. But under the idea of the law of nations they do not wish this, and reject in practice what is correct in theory. If all

visitor that one may demand. A special beneficent agreement would be needed in order to give an outsider a right to become a fellow inhabitant for a certain length of time. It is only a right of temporary sojourn, a right to associate, which all men have. They have it by virtue of their common possession of the surface of the earth, where, as a globe, they cannot infinitely disperse and hence must finally tolerate the presence of each other. Originally, no one had more right than another to a particular part of the earth.

Uninhabitable parts of the earth—the sea and the deserts—divide this community of all men, but the ship and the camel (the desert ship) enable them to approach each other across these unruled regions and to establish communication by using the common right to the face of the earth, which belongs to human beings generally. The inhospitality of the inhabitants of coasts (for instance, of the Barbary Coast) in robbing ships in neighboring seas or enslaving stranded travelers, or the inhospitality of the inhabitants of the deserts (for instance, the Bedouin Arabs) who view contact with nomadic tribes as conferring the right to plunder them, is thus opposed to natural law, even though it extends the right of hospitality, i.e., the privilege of foreign arrivals, no further than to conditions of the possibility of seeking to communicate with the prior inhabitants. In this way distant parts of the world can come into peaceable relations with each other, and these are finally publicly established by law. Thus the human race can gradually be brought closer and closer to a constitution establishing world citizenship.

But to this perfection compare the inhospitable actions of the civilized and especially of the commercial states of our part of the world. The injustice which they show to lands and peoples they visit (which is equivalent to conquering them) is carried by them to terrifying lengths. America, the lands inhabited by the Negro, the Spice Islands, the Cape, etc., were at the time of their discovery considered by these civilized intruders as lands without owners, for they counted the inhabitants as nothing. In East India (Hindustan), under the pretense of establishing economic undertakings, they brought in foreign soldiers and used them to oppress the natives, excited widespread wars among the various states, spread famine, rebellion, perfidy, and the whole litany of evils which afflict mankind.

China [10] and Japan (Nippon), who have had experience

[10] To call this great empire by the name it gives itself, namely "China" and not "Sina" or anything like that, we have only to refer to [A.] Georgi, *Alphabetum Tibetanum*, pp. 651-54, especially note b. According to the note of Professor [Johann Eberhard] Fischer of Petersburg, there is no definite word used in that country as its name; the most usual word is "Kin," i.e., gold (which the Tibetans call "Ser"). Accordingly, the emperor is called "the king of gold," that is, king of the most splendid country in the world. In the empire itself, this word may be pronounced *Chin,* while because of the guttural sound the Italian missionaries may have called it *Kin.*—It is clear that what the Romans called the "Land of Seres" was China; the silk, however, was sent to Europe across Greater Tibet (through Lesser Tibet, Bukhara, Persia, and then on).

This suggests many reflections concerning the antiquity of this wonderful state, in comparison with that of Hindustan at the time of its union with Tibet and thence with Japan. We see, on the contrary, that the name "Sina" or "Tshina," said to have been used by the neighbors of the country, suggests nothing.

Perhaps we can also explain the very ancient but never well-known intercourse of Europe with Tibet by considering the shout, Κονξ 'Ομπαξ ("*Konx Ompax*"), of the hierophants in the Eleusinian mysteries, as we learn from Hysichius (cf. *Travels of the Young Anacharsis,* Part V, p. 447 ff.). For, according to Georgi, *op. cit.,* the word *Concoia* means God, which has a striking resemblance to *Konx. Pah-cio* (*ibid.,* 520), which the Greeks may well have pronounced *pax,* means the *promulgator legis,* divinity pervading the whole of nature (also called *Cencresi,* p. 177). *Om,* however, which La Croze translates as *benedictus* ("blessed"), when applied to divinity perhaps means "the beatified" (p. 507). P. Franz Orazio often asked the Lamas of Tibet what they understood by "God" (*Concoia*) and always got the answer, "It is the assembly of saints" (i.e., the assembly of the blessed ones who, according to the doctrine of rebirth, finally, after many wanderings through bodies of all kinds, have returned to God, or *Burchane;* that is to say, they are transmigrated souls, beings to be worshiped, p.

with such guests, have wisely refused them entry, the former permitting their approach to their shores but not their entry, while the latter permit this approach to only one European people, the Dutch, but treat them like prisoners, not allowing them any communication with the inhabitants. The worst of this (or, to speak with the moralist, the best) is that all these outrages profit them nothing, since all these commercial ventures stand on the verge of collapse, and the Sugar Islands, that place of the most refined and cruel slavery, produces no real revenue except indirectly, only serving a not very praiseworthy purpose of furnishing sailors for war fleets and thus for the conduct of war in Europe. This service is rendered to powers which make a great show of their piety, and, while they drink injustice like water, they regard themselves as the elect in point of orthodoxy.

Since the narrower or wider community of the peoples of the earth has developed so far that a violation of rights in one place is felt throughout the world, the idea of a law of world citizenship is no high-flown or exaggerated notion. It is a supplement to the unwritten code of the civil and international law, indispensable for the maintenance of the public human rights and hence also of perpetual peace. One cannot flatter oneself into believing one can approach this peace except under the condition outlined here.

---

223). That mysterious expression *Konx Ompax* may well mean "the holy" (*Konx*), the blessed (*Om*), the wise (*Pax*), the supreme being pervading the world (nature personified). Its use in the Greek mysteries may indicate monotheism among the epopts in contrast to the polytheism of the people (though Orazio scented atheism there). How that mysterious word came to the Greeks via Tibet can perhaps be explained in this way; and the early traffic of Europe with China, also through Tibet, and perhaps earlier than communication with Hindustan, is made probable.

FIRST SUPPLEMENT

OF THE GUARANTEE FOR PERPETUAL PEACE

The guarantee of perpetual peace is nothing less than that great artist, nature (*natura daedala rerum*). In her mechanical course we see that her aim is to produce a harmony among men, against their will and indeed through their discord. As a necessity working according to laws we do not know, we call it destiny. But, considering its design in world history, we call it "providence," inasmuch as we discern in it the profound wisdom of a higher cause which predetermines the course of nature and directs it to the objective final end of the human race.[1] We do not observe or

[1] In the mechanism of nature, to which man belongs as a sensuous being, a form is exhibited which is basic to its existence; we can conceive of this form only as dependent upon the end to which the Author of the world has previously destined it. This predetermination we call "divine providence" generally, and so far as it is exercised at the beginning of the world we call it "founding providence" (*Providentia conditrix; semel iussit, semper parent*—AUGUSTINE).* As maintaining nature in its course by universal laws of design, it is called "ruling providence" (*providentia gubernatrix*); as directing nature to ends not foreseen by man and only conjectured from the actual result, it is called "guiding providence" (*providentia directrix*). With respect to single events as divine ends, it is no longer called "providence" but "dispensation" (*directio extraordinaria*). But since "divine dispensation" indicates miracles, even if the events themselves are not called such, it is a foolish pretension of man to wish to interpret them as such, since it is absurd to infer from a single event to a particular principle of the efficient cause, namely, that this event is an end and not merely a mechanical corollary of another end wholly unknown to us. However pious and humble such talk may be, it is full of self-conceit. The division of providence, considered not formally but materially, i.e., with respect to objects in the world to which it is directed, into either general or particular providence, is false and

* ["Providence is a founder; once she orders, they always obey."]

infer this providence in the cunning contrivances of nature, but, as in questions of the relation of the form of things to ends in general, we can and must supply it from our own minds in order to conceive of its possibility by analogy to actions of human art. The idea of the relation-

---

self-contradictory. (This division appears, for instance, in the statement that providence cares for the preservation of the species but leaves individuals to chance.) It is contradictory because it is called universal in its purpose, and therefore no single thing can be excluded from it. Presumably, therefore, a formal distinction is intended, according to the way in which providence seeks its ends. This is the distinction between the ordinary and the special ways of providence. (Under the former we may cite the annual dying-out and rebirth of nature with the changes of the season; under the latter, the transport of wood by ocean currents to arctic lands where it cannot grow, yet where it is needed by the inhabitants who could not live without it.) Although we can very well explain the physico-mechanical cause of these extraordinary cases (e.g., by reference to the wooded banks of rivers in temperate lands, the falling of trees into the rivers, and then their being carried along by the Gulf Stream), we must not overlook the teleological cause, which intimates the foresight of a wisdom commanding over nature.

The concept of intervention or concurrence (*concursus*) in producing an effect in the world of sense must be given up, though it is quite usual in the schools. For to try to pair the disparate (*gryphes iungere equis*),† and to let that which is itself the perfect cause of events in the world supplement its own predetermining providence in the course of the world (which would therefore have to have been inadequate), is self-contradictory. We fall into this self-contradiction, for example, when we say that next to God it was the physician who cured the ill, as if God had been his helper. For *causa solitaria non iuvat;* God is the author of the physician and all his medicines, and if we insist on ascending to the highest but theoretically inconceivable first cause, the effect must be ascribed entirely to Him. Or we can ascribe it entirely to the physician, so far as we consider the occurrence as explicable in a chain of causes under the order of nature.

But, besides being self-contradictory, such a mode of thought brings an end to all definite principles in judging an effect. In a morally practical point of view, however, which is directed exclusively to the supersensuous, the concept of the divine *concursus* is quite suitable and even necessary. We find this, for instance, in the belief that God

† ["Griffins shall mate with mares."—An allusion to Virgil, *Eclogue* VIII.]

ship and harmony between these actions and the end which reason directly assigns to us is transcendent from a theoretical point of view; from a practical standpoint, with respect, for example, to the ideal of perpetual peace, the concept is dogmatic and its reality is well established, and thus the mechanism of nature may be employed to that end. The use of the word "nature" is more fitting to the limits of human reason and more modest than an expression indicating a providence unknown to us. This is especially true when we are dealing with questions of theory and not of religion, as at present, for human reason in questions of the relation of effects to their causes must remain within the limits of possible experience. On the other hand, the use of the word "providence" here intimates the possession of wings like those of Icarus, conducting us toward the secret of its unfathomable purpose.

Before we more narrowly define the guarantee which nature gives, it is necessary to examine the situation in which she has placed her actors on her vast stage, a situation which finally assures peace among them. Then we shall see how she accomplishes the latter. Her preparatory arrangements are:

1. In every region of the world she has made it possible for men to live.
2. By war she has driven them even into the most inhospitable regions in order to populate them.
3. By the same means, she has forced them into more or less lawful relations with each other.

That in the cold wastes by the Arctic Ocean the moss grows which the reindeer digs from the snow in order to

will compensate for our own lack of justice, provided our intention was genuine; that He will do so by means that are inconceivable to us, and that therefore we should not relent in our endeavor after the good. But it is self-evident that no one should try to explain a good action (as an event in the world) as a result of this *concursus*, for this would be a vain theoretical knowledge of the supersensuous and therefore absurd.

make itself the prey or the conveyance of the Ostyak or Samoyed; or that the saline sandy deserts are inhabited by the camel which appears created as it were in order that they might not go unused—that is already wonderful. Still clearer is the end when we see how besides the furry animals of the Arctic there are also the seal, the walrus, and the whale which afford the inhabitants food from their flesh and warmth from their blubber. But the care of nature excites the greatest wonder when we see how she brings wood (though the inhabitants do not know whence it comes) to these barren climates, without which they would have neither canoes, weapons, nor huts, and when we see how these natives are so occupied with their war against the animals that they live in peace with each other —but what drove them there was presumably nothing else than war.

The first instrument of war among the animals which man learned to tame and to domesticate was the horse (for the elephant belongs to later times, to the luxury of already established states). The art of cultivating certain types of plants (grain) whose original characteristics we do not know, and the increase and improvement of fruits by transplantation and grafting (in Europe perhaps only the crab apple and the wild pear), could arise only under conditions prevailing in already established states where property was secure. Before this could take place, it was necessary that men who had first subsisted in anarchic freedom by hunting,[2] fishing, and sheepherding should have been

2 Among all modes of life there is undoubtedly none more opposed to a civilized constitution than that of hunting, because families which must dwell separately soon become strangers and, scattered in extensive forests, also enemies, since each needs a great deal of space for obtaining food and clothing. The Noachic ban on blood (Genesis 9:4-6) (which was imposed by the baptized Jews as a condition on the later Christians who were converted from heathenism, though in a different connection—see The Acts 15:20; 21:25) seems to have been originally nothing more than a prohibition against the hunting life, because here raw flesh must often have been eaten; when the latter was forbidden, so also was the former.

forced into an agricultural life. Then salt and iron were discovered. These were perhaps the first articles of commerce for the various peoples and were sought far and wide; in this way a peaceful traffic among nations was established, and thus understanding, conventions, and peaceable relations were established among the most distant peoples.

As nature saw to it that men *could* live everywhere in the world, she also despotically willed that they *should* do so, even against their inclination and without this *ought* being based on a concept of duty to which they were bound by a moral law. She chose war as the means to this end. So we see peoples whose common language shows that they have a common origin. For instance, the Samoyeds on the Arctic Ocean and a people with a similar language a thousand miles away in the Altaian Mountains are separated by a Mongolian people adept at horsemanship and hence at war; the latter drove the former into the most inhospitable arctic regions where they certainly would not have spread of their own accord.[3] Again, it is the same with the Finns who in the most northerly part of Europe are called Lapps; Goths and Sarmatians have separated them from the Hungarians to whom they are related in language. What can have driven the Eskimos, a race entirely distinct from all others in America and perhaps descended from primeval European adventurers, so far into the North, or the Pescherais as far south as Tierra del Fuego, if it were not war which nature uses to populate the whole earth? War itself requires no special motive but

[3] One could ask: If nature willed that these icy coasts should not remain uninhabited, what would become of the inhabitants if nature ever failed (as might be expected) to bring driftwood to them? For it is reasonable to believe that, in the progress of civilization, the occupants of the temperate zone would make better use of the wood along rivers than simply to let it fall into the water and be carried to the sea. I answer: If nature compels them to peace, the dwellers along the Ob, the Yenisei, or the Lena will bring it to them, exchanging it for animal products in which the sea around the Arctic coasts abounds.

appears to be engrafted on human nature; it passes even for something noble, to which the love of glory impels men quite apart from any selfish urges. Thus among the American savages, just as much as among those of Europe during the age of chivalry, military valor is held to be of great worth in itself, not only during war (which is natural) but in order that there should be war. Often war is waged only in order to show valor; thus an inner dignity is ascribed to war itself, and even some philosophers have praised it as an ennoblement of humanity, forgetting the pronouncement of the Greek who said, "War is an evil inasmuch as it produces more wicked men than it takes away." So much for the measures nature takes to lead the human race, considered as a class of animals, to her own end.

Now we come to the question concerning that which is most essential in the design of perpetual peace: What has nature done with regard to this end which man's own reason makes his duty? That is, what has nature done to favor man's moral purpose, and how has she guaranteed (by compulsion but without prejudice to his freedom) that he shall do that which he ought to but does not do under the laws of freedom? This question refers to all three phases of public law, namely, civil law, the law of nations, and the law of world citizenship. If I say of nature that she wills that this or that occur, I do not mean that she imposes a duty on us to do it, for this can be done only by free practical reason; rather I mean that she herself does it, whether we will or not (*fata volentem ducunt, nolentem trahunt*).[4]

1. Even if a people were not forced by internal discord to submit to public laws, war would compel them to do so, for we have already seen that nature has placed each people near another which presses upon it, and against this it must form itself into a state in order to defend itself. Now the republican constitution is the only one entirely fitting to the rights of man. But it is the most difficult to estab-

---

4 ["Fates lead the willing, drive the unwilling" (Seneca *Epist. mor.* XVIII. 4).]

lish and even harder to preserve, so that many [5] say a republic would have to be a nation of angels, because men with their selfish inclinations are not capable of a constitution of such sublime form. But precisely with these inclinations nature comes to the aid of the general will established on reason, which is revered even though impotent in practice. Thus it is only a question of a good organization of the state (which does lie in man's power), whereby the powers of each selfish inclination are so arranged in opposition that one moderates or destroys the ruinous effect of the other. The consequence for reason is the same as if none of them existed, and man is forced to be a good citizen even if not a morally good person.

The problem of organizing a state, however hard it may seem, can be solved even for a race of devils, if only they are intelligent. The problem is: "Given a multitude of rational beings requiring universal laws for their preservation, but each of whom is secretly inclined to exempt himself from them, to establish a constitution in such a way that, although their private intentions conflict, they check each other, with the result that their public conduct is the same as if they had no such intentions."

A problem like this must be capable of solution; it does not require that we know how to attain the moral improvement of men but only that we should know the mechanism of nature in order to use it on men, organizing the conflict of the hostile intentions present in a people in such a way that they must compel themselves to submit to coercive laws. Thus a state of peace is established in which laws have force. We can see, even in actual states, which are far from perfectly organized, that in their foreign relations they approach that which the idea of right prescribes. This is so in spite of the fact that the intrinsic element of morality is certainly not the cause of it. (A good constitution is not to be expected from morality, but, conversely, a

---

[5] [E.g., Rousseau, *Social Contract*, Book III, chap. 4.]

good moral condition of a people is to be expected only under a good constitution.) Instead of genuine morality, the mechanism of nature brings it to pass through selfish inclinations, which naturally conflict outwardly but which can be used by reason as a means for its own end, the sovereignty of law, and, as concerns the state, for promoting and securing internal and external peace.

This, then, is the truth of the matter: Nature inexorably wills that the right should finally triumph. What we neglect to do comes about by itself, though with great inconveniences to us. "If you bend the reed too much, you break it; and he who attempts too much attempts nothing" (Bouterwek).[6]

2. The idea of international law presupposes the separate existence of many independent but neighboring states. Although this condition is itself a state of war (unless a federative union prevents the outbreak of hostilities), this is rationally preferable to the amalgamation of states under one superior power, as this would end in one universal monarchy, and laws always lose in vigor what government gains in extent; hence a soulless despotism falls into anarchy after stifling the seeds of the good. Nevertheless, every state, or its ruler, desires to establish lasting peace in this way, aspiring if possible to rule the whole world. But nature wills otherwise. She employs two means to separate peoples and to prevent them from mixing: differences of language and of religion.[7] These differences involve a tendency to mutual hatred and pretexts for war, but the prog-

---

6 [Friedrich Bouterwek (1766-1828).]

7 Difference of religion—a singular expression! It is precisely as if one spoke of different moralities. There may very well be different kinds of historical faiths attached to different means employed in the promotion of religion, and they belong merely in the field of learned investigation. Similarly there may be different religious texts (Zendavesta, the Veda, the Koran, etc.), but such differences do not exist in religion, there being only one religion valid for all men and in all ages. These can, therefore, be nothing else than accidental vehicles of religion, thus changing with times and places.

ress of civilization and men's gradual approach to greater harmony in their principles finally leads to peaceful agreement. This is not like that peace which despotism (in the burial ground of freedom) produces through a weakening of all powers; it is, on the contrary, produced and maintained by their equilibrium in liveliest competition.

3. Just as nature wisely separates nations, which the will of every state, sanctioned by the principles of international law, would gladly unite by artifice or force, nations which could not have secured themselves against violence and war by means of the law of world citizenship unite because of mutual interest. The spirit of commerce, which is incompatible with war, sooner or later gains the upper hand in every state. As the power of money is perhaps the most dependable of all the powers (means) included under the state power, states see themselves forced, without any moral urge, to promote honorable peace and by mediation to prevent war wherever it threatens to break out. They do so exactly as if they stood in perpetual alliances, for great offensive alliances are in the nature of the case rare and even less often successful.

In this manner nature guarantees perpetual peace by the mechanism of human passions. Certainly she does not do so with sufficient certainty for us to predict the future in any theoretical sense, but adequately from a practical point of view, making it our duty to work toward this end, which is not just a chimerical one.

SECOND SUPPLEMENT

SECRET ARTICLE FOR PERPETUAL PEACE

A secret article in contracts under public law is objectively, i.e., from the standpoint of its content, a contradiction. Subjectively, however, a secret clause can be present in them, because the persons who dictate it might find it compromising to their dignity to declare openly that they are its authors.

The only article of this kind is contained in the statement: "The opinions of philosophers on the conditions of the possibility of public peace shall be consulted by those states armed for war."

But it appears humiliating to the legislative authority of a state, to whom we must naturally attribute the utmost wisdom, to seek instruction from subjects (the philosophers) on principles of conduct toward other states. It is nevertheless very advisable to do so. Therefore, the state tacitly and secretly invites them to give their opinions, that is, the state will let them publicly and freely talk about the general maxims of warfare and of the establishment of peace (for they will do that of themselves, provided they are not forbidden to do so). It does not require a particular convention among states to see that this is done, since their agreement on this point lies in an obligation already established by universal human reason which is morally legislative.

I do not mean that the state should give the principles of philosophers any preference over the decisions of lawyers (the representatives of the state power); I only ask that they be given a hearing. The lawyer, who has made not only the scales of right but also the sword of justice his symbol, generally uses the latter not merely to keep back all foreign influences from the former, but, if the scale does not sink the way he wishes, he also throws the sword into it (*vae victis*), a practice to which he often has the greatest temptation because he is not also a philosopher, even in morality. His office is only to apply positive laws, not to inquire whether they might not need improvement. The administrative function, which is the lower one in his faculty, he counts as the higher because it is invested with power (as is the case also with the other faculties [of medicine and theology]).[1] The philosophical faculty occupies a very low rank against this allied power. Thus it is said of philosophy, for example, that she is the handmaiden to theology, and the other faculties claim as much. But one does not see distinctly whether she precedes her mistress with a flambeau or follows bearing her train.

That kings should philosophize or philosophers become kings is not to be expected. Nor is it to be wished, since the possession of power inevitably corrupts the untrammeled judgment of reason. But kings or kinglike peoples which rule themselves under laws of equality should not suffer the class of philosophers to disappear or to be silent, but should let them speak openly. This is indispensable to the enlightenment of the business of government, and, since the class of philosophers is by nature incapable of plotting and lobbying, it is above suspicion of being made up of propagandists.

[1] [Kant is here referring to the rivalry among the four faculties of the German university of his time, viz., philosophy, theology, law, and medicine. Cf. his *Strife of the Faculties*.]

APPENDIX I

ON THE OPPOSITION BETWEEN MORAL-ITY AND POLITICS WITH RESPECT TO PERPETUAL PEACE

Taken objectively, morality is in itself practical, being the totality of unconditionally mandatory laws according to which we ought to act. It would obviously be absurd, after granting authority to the concept of duty, to pretend that we cannot do our duty, for in that case this concept would itself drop out of morality (*ultra posse nemo obligatur*). Consequently, there can be no conflict of politics, as a practical doctrine of right, with ethics, as a theoretical doctrine of right. That is to say, there is no conflict of practice with theory, unless by ethics we mean a general doctrine of prudence, which would be the same as a theory of the maxims for choosing the most fitting means to accomplish the purposes of self-interest. But to give this meaning to ethics is equivalent to denying that there is any such thing at all.

Politics says, "Be ye wise as serpents"; morality adds, as a limiting condition, "and guileless as doves." If these two injunctions are incompatible in a single command, then politics and morality are really in conflict; but if these two qualities ought always to be united, the thought of contrariety is absurd, and the question as to how the conflict between morals and politics is to be resolved cannot even be posed as a problem. Although the proposition, "Honesty is the best policy," implies a theory which practice unfortunately often refutes, the equally theoretical "Honesty is better than any policy" is beyond refutation and is indeed the indispensable condition of policy.

The tutelary divinity of morality yields not to Jupiter,

for this tutelary divinity of force still is subject to destiny. That is, reason is not yet sufficiently enlightened to survey the entire series of predetermining causes, and such vision would be necessary for one to be able to foresee with certainty the happy or unhappy effects which follow human actions by the mechanism of nature (though we know enough to have hope that they will accord with our wishes). But what we have to do in order to remain in the path of duty (according to rules of wisdom) reason instructs us by her rules, and her teaching suffices for attaining the ultimate end.

Now the practical man, to whom morality is mere theory even though he concedes that it can and should be followed, ruthlessly renounces our fond hope [that it will be followed]. He does so because he pretends to have seen in advance that man, by his nature, will never will what is required for realizing the goal of perpetual peace. Certainly the will of each individual to live under a juridical constitution according to principles of freedom (i.e., the distributive unity of the will of all) is not sufficient to this end. That all together should will this condition (i.e., the collective unity of the united will)—the solution to this troublous problem—is also required. Thus a whole of civil society is formed. But since a uniting cause must supervene upon the variety of particular volitions in order to produce a common will from them, establishing this whole is something no one individual in the group can perform; hence in the practical execution of this idea we can count on nothing but force to establish the juridical condition, on the compulsion of which public law will later be established. We can scarcely hope to find in the legislator a moral intention sufficient to induce him to commit to the general will the establishment of a legal constitution after he has formed the nation from a horde of savages; therefore, we cannot but expect (in practice) to find in execution wide deviations from this idea (in theory).

It will then be said that he who once has power in his

hands will not allow the people to prescribe laws for him; a state which once is able to stand under no external laws will not submit to the decision of other states how it should seek its rights against them; and one continent, which feels itself superior to another, even though the other does not interfere with it, will not neglect to increase its power by robbery or even conquest. Thus all theoretical plans of civil and international laws and laws of world citizenship vanish into empty and impractical ideas, while practice based on empirical principles of human nature, not blushing to draw its maxims from the usages of the world, can alone hope to find a sure ground for its political edifice.

If there is no freedom and no morality based on freedom, and everything which occurs or can occur happens by the mere mechanism of nature, certainly politics (which is the art of using this mechanism for ruling men) is the whole of practical wisdom, and the concept of right is an empty thought. But if we find it necessary to connect the latter with politics, and even to raise it to a limiting condition thereon, the possibility of their being united must be conceded. I can easily conceive of a moral politician, i.e., one who so chooses political principles that they are consistent with those of morality; but I cannot conceive of a political moralist, one who forges a morality in such a way that it conforms to the statesman's advantage.

When a remediable defect is found in the constitution of the state or in its relations to others, the principle of the moral politician will be that it is a duty, especially of the rulers of the state, to inquire how it can be remedied as soon as possible in a way conforming to natural law as a model presented by reason; this he will do even if it costs self-sacrifice. But it would be absurd to demand that every defect be immediately and impetuously changed, since the disruption of the bonds of a civil society or a union of world citizens before a better constitution is ready to take its place is against all politics agreeing with morality. But it can be demanded that at least the maxim of the necessity of such a change should be taken to heart by those in power, so that they may continuously approach the goal of the constitution that is best under laws of right. A state may exercise a republican rule, even though by its present constitution it has a despotic sovereignty, until gradually the people becomes susceptible to the influence simply of the idea of the authority of law (as if it possessed physical power) and thus is found fit to be its own legislator (as its own legislation is originally established on law). If a violent revolution, engendered by a bad constitution, introduces by illegal means a more legal constitution, to lead the people back to the earlier constitution would not be permitted; but, while the revolution lasted, each person who openly or covertly shared in it would have justly incurred the punishment due to those who rebel. As to the external relations of states, a state cannot be expected to renounce its constitution even though it is a despotic one (which has the advantage of being stronger in relation to foreign enemies) so long as it is exposed to the danger of being swallowed up by other states. Thus even in the case of the intention to improve the constitution, postponement to a more propitious time may be permitted.[1]

It may be that despotizing moralists, in practice blundering, often violate rules of political prudence through measures they adopt or propose too precipitately; but experi-

---

[1] These are permissive laws of reason. Public law laden with injustice must be allowed to stand, either until everything is of itself ripe for complete reform or until this maturity has been brought about by peaceable means; for a legal constitution, even though it be right to only a low degree, is better than none at all, the anarchic condition which would result from precipitate reform. Political wisdom, therefore, will make it a duty to introduce reforms which accord with the ideal of public law. But even when nature herself produces revolutions, political wisdom will not employ them to legitimize still greater oppression. On the contrary, it will use them as a call of nature for fundamental reforms to produce a lawful constitution founded upon principles of freedom, for only such a constitution is durable.

ence will gradually retrieve them from their infringement of nature and lead them on to a better course. But the moralizing politician, by glossing over principles of politics which are opposed to the right with the pretext that human nature is not capable of the good as reason prescribes it, only makes reform impossible and perpetuates the violation of law.

Instead of possessing the *practical science* they boast of, these politicians have only *practices;* they flatter the power which is then ruling so as not to be remiss in their private advantage, and they sacrifice the nation and, possibly, the whole world. This is the way of all professional lawyers (not legislators) when they go into politics. Their task is not to reason too nicely about the legislation but to execute the momentary commands on the statute books; consequently, the legal constitution in force at any time is to them the best, but when it is amended from above, this amendment always seems best, too. Thus everything is preserved in its accustomed mechanical order. Their adroitness in fitting into all circumstances gives them the illusion of being able to judge constitutional principles according to concepts of right (not empirically, but a priori). They make a great show of understanding *men* (which is certainly something to be expected of them, since they have to deal with so many) without understanding *man* and what can be made of him, for they lack the higher point of view of anthropological observation which is needed for this. If with these ideas they go into civil and international law, as reason prescribes it, they take this step in a spirit of chicanery, for they still follow their accustomed mechanical routine of despotically imposed coercive laws in a field where only concepts of reason can establish a legal compulsion according to the principles of freedom, under which alone a just and durable constitution is possible. In this field the pretended practical man thinks he can solve the problem of establishing such a constitution without the rational idea but solely from the experience he has had with what was previously the most lasting constitution—a constitution which in many cases was opposed to the right.

The maxims which he makes use of (though he does not divulge them) are, roughly speaking, the following sophisms:

1. *Fac et excusa.* Seize every favorable opportunity for usurping the right of the state over its own people or over a neighboring people; the justification will be easier and more elegant *ex post facto,* and the power can be more easily glossed over, especially when the supreme power in the state is also the legislative authority which must be obeyed without argument. It is much more difficult to do the violence when one has first to wait upon the consideration of convincing arguments and to meet them with counterarguments. Boldness itself gives the appearance of inner conviction of the legitimacy of the deed, and the god of success is afterward the best advocate.

2. *Si fecisti, nega.* What you have committed, deny that it was your fault—for instance, that you have brought your people to despair and hence to rebellion. Rather assert that it was due to the obstinacy of your subjects; or, if you have conquered a neighboring nation, say that the fault lies in the nature of man, who, if not met by force, can be counted on to make use of it to conquer you.

3. *Divide et impera.* That is, if there are certain privileged persons in your nation who have chosen you as their chief (*primus inter pares*), set them at variance with one another and embroil them with the people. Show the latter visions of greater freedom, and all will soon depend on your untrammeled will. Or if it is foreign states that concern you, it is a pretty safe means to sow discord among them so that, by seeming to protect the weaker, you can conquer them one after another.

Certainly no one is now the dupe of these political maxims, for they are already universally known. Nor are they blushed at, as if their injustice were too glaring, for great powers blush only at the judgment of other great powers but not at that of the common masses. It is not that they are ashamed of revealing such principles (for all of them are in the same boat with respect to the morality of their maxims); they are ashamed only when these maxims fail, for they still have political honor which cannot be disputed—and this honor is the aggrandizement of their power by whatever means.[2]

All these twistings and turnings of an immoral doctrine of prudence in leading men from their natural state of war to a state of peace prove at least that men in both their private and their public relationships cannot reject the concept of right or trust themselves openly to establish politics merely on the artifices of prudence. Thus they do not refuse obedience to the concept of public law, which is especially manifest in international law; on the contrary,

[2] Even if we doubt a certain wickedness in the nature of men who live together in a state, and instead plausibly cite lack of civilization, which is not yet sufficiently advanced, i.e., regard barbarism as the cause of those antilawful manifestations of their character, this viciousness is clearly and incontestably shown in the foreign relations of states. Within each state it is veiled by the compulsion of civil laws, because the inclination to violence between the citizens is fettered by the stronger power of the government. This relationship not only gives a moral veneer (*causae non causae*) to the whole but actually facilitates the development of the moral disposition to a direct respect for the law by placing a barrier against the outbreak of unlawful inclinations. Each person believes that he himself would hold the concept of law sacred and faithfully follow it provided he were sure that he could expect the same from others, and the government does in part assure him of this. Thereby a great step (though not yet a moral step) is taken toward morality, which is attachment to this concept of duty for its own sake and without regard to hope of a similar response from others. But since each one with his own good opinion of himself presupposes a malicious disposition on the part of all the others, they all pronounce the judgment that they in fact are all worth very little. We shall not discuss how this comes about, though it cannot be blamed on the nature of man as a free being. But since even respect for the concept of right (which man cannot absolutely refuse to respect) solemnly sanctions the theory that he has the capacity of conforming to it, everyone sees that he, for his part, must act according to it, however others may act.

they give all due honor to it, even when they are inventing a hundred pretenses and subterfuges to escape from it in practice, imputing its authority, as the source and union of all laws, to crafty force.

Let us put an end to this sophism, if not to the injustice it protects, and force the false representatives of power to confess that they do not plead in favor of the right but in favor of might. This is revealed in the imperious tone they assume as if they themselves could command the right. Let us remove the delusion by which they and others are duped, and discover the supreme principle from which the intention to perpetual peace stems. Let us show that everything evil which stands in its way derives from the fact that the political moralist begins where the moral politician would correctly leave off, and that, since he thus subordinates principles to the end (putting the cart before the horse), he vitiates his own purpose of bringing politics into agreement with morality.

To make practical philosophy self-consistent, it is necessary, first, to decide the question: In problems of practical reason, must we begin from its material principles, i.e., the end as the object of choice? Or should we begin from the formal principles of pure reason, i.e., from the principle which is concerned solely with freedom in outer relations and which reads, "So act that you can will that your maxim could become a universal law, regardless of the end"?

Without doubt it is the latter which has precedence, for as a principle of law it has unconditional necessity. On the other hand, the former is obligatory only if we presuppose the empirical conditions of the proposed end, i.e., its practicability. Thus if this end (in this case, perpetual peace) is a duty, it must be derived from the formal principle of the maxims of external actions. The first principle, that of the political moralist, pertaining to civil and international law and the law of world citizenship, is merely a problem of technique (*problema technicum*); the second, as the prob-

lem of the moral politician to whom it is an ethical problem (*problema morale*), is far removed from the other in
its method of leading toward perpetual peace, which is
wished not merely as a material good but also as a condition issuing from an acknowledgment of duty.

For the solution of the former, the problem of political
prudence, much knowledge of nature is required so that its
mechanism may be employed toward the desired end; yet
all this is uncertain in its results for perpetual peace, with
whatever sphere of public law we are concerned. It is uncertain, for example, whether the people are better kept in
obedience and maintained in prosperity by severity or by
the charm of distinctions which flatter their vanity, by the
power of one or the union of various chiefs, or perhaps
merely by a serving nobility or by the power of the people.
History furnishes us with contradictory examples from all
governments (with the exception of the truly republican,
which can alone appeal to the mind of a moral politician).
Still more uncertain is an international law allegedly
erected on the statutes of ministries. It is, in fact, a word
without meaning, resting as it does on compacts which, in
the very act of being concluded, contain secret reservations
for their violation.

On the other hand, the solution of the second problem,
that of political wisdom, presses itself upon us, as it were;
it is clear to everyone and puts to shame all affectation. It
leads directly to the end, but, remembering discretion, it
does not precipitately hasten to do so by force; rather, it
continuously approaches it under the conditions offered by
favorable circumstances.

Then it may be said, "Seek ye first the kingdom of pure
practical reason and its righteousness, and your end (the
blessing of perpetual peace) will necessarily follow." For it
is the peculiarity of morals, especially with respect to its
principles of public law and hence in relation to a politics
known a priori, that the less it makes conduct depend on
the proposed end, i.e., the intended material or moral ad-

vantage, the more it agrees with it in general. This is because it is the universal will given a priori (in a nation or in the relations among different nations) which determines the law among men, and if practice consistently follows it, this will can also, by the mechanism of nature, cause the desired result and make the concept of law effective. So, for instance, it is a principle of moral politics that a people should unite into a state according to juridical concepts of freedom and equality, and this principle is based not on prudence but on duty. Political moralists may argue as much as they wish about the natural mechanism of a mass of men forming a society, assuming a mechanism which would weaken those principles and vitiate their end; or they may seek to prove their assertions by examples of poorly organized constitutions of ancient and modern times (for instance, of democracies without representative systems). They deserve no hearing, particularly as such a pernicious theory may itself occasion the evil which it prophesies, throwing human beings into one class with all other living machines, differing from them only in their consciousness that they are not free, which makes them, in their own judgment, the most miserable of all beings in the world.

The true but somewhat boastful sentence which has become proverbial, *Fiat iustitia, pereat mundus* ("Let justice reign even if all the rascals in the world should perish from it"), is a stout principle of right which cuts asunder the whole tissue of artifice or force. But it should not be misunderstood as a permission to use one's own right with extreme rigor (which would conflict with ethical duty); it should be understood as the obligation of those in power not to limit or to extend anyone's right through sympathy or disfavor. This requires, first, an internal constitution of the state erected on pure principles of right, and, second, a convention of the state with other near or distant states (analogous to a universal state) for the legal settlement of their differences. This implies only that political maxims must not be derived from the welfare or happiness which a single state expects from obedience to them, and thus not from the end which one of them proposes for itself. That is, they must not be deduced from volition as the supreme yet empirical principle of political wisdom, but rather from the pure concept of the duty of right, from the *ought* whose principle is given a priori by pure reason, regardless of what the physical consequences may be. The world will by no means perish by a diminution in the number of evil men. Moral evil has the indiscerptible property of being opposed to and destructive of its own purposes (especially in the relationships between evil men); thus it gives place to the moral principle of the good, though only through a slow progress.

Thus objectively, or in theory, there is no conflict between morals and politics. Subjectively, however, in the selfish propensity of men (which should not be called "practice," as this would imply that it rested on rational maxims), this conflict will always remain. Indeed, it should remain, because it serves as a whetstone of virtue, whose true courage (by the principle, *tu ne cede malis, sed contra audentior ito*) [3] in the present case does not so much consist in defying with strong resolve evils and sacrifices which must be undertaken along with the conflict, but rather in detecting and conquering the crafty and far more dangerously deceitful and treasonable principle of evil in ourselves, which puts forward the weakness of human nature as justification for every transgression.

In fact, the political moralist may say: The ruler and people, or nation and nation, do each other no injustice when by violence or fraud they make war on each other, although they do commit injustice in general in that they refuse to respect the concept of right, which alone could establish perpetual peace. For since the one does transgress his duty against the other, who is likewise lawlessly disposed toward him, each gets what he deserves when they

[3] ["Yield not to evils, but go against the stronger" (*Aeneid* VI. 95).]

destroy each other. But enough of the race still remains to let this game continue into the remotest ages in order that posterity, some day, might take these perpetrators as a warning example. Hence providence is justified in the history of the world, for the moral principle in man is never extinguished, while with advancing civilization reason grows pragmatically in its capacity to realize ideas of law. But at the same time the culpability for the transgressions also grows. If we assume that humanity never will or can be improved, the only thing which a theodicy seems unable to justify is creation itself, the fact that a race of such corrupt beings ever was on earth. But the point of view necessary for such an assumption is far too high for us, and we cannot theoretically support our philosophical concepts of the supreme power which is inscrutable to us.

To such dubious consequences we are inevitably driven if we do not assume that pure principles of right have objective reality, i.e., that they may be applied, and that the people in a state and, further, states themselves in their mutual relations should act according to them, whatever objections empirical politics may raise. Thus true politics can never take a step without rendering homage to morality. Though politics by itself is a difficult art, its union with morality is no art at all, for this union cuts the knot which politics could not untie when they were in conflict. The rights of men must be held sacred, however much sacrifice it may cost the ruling power. One cannot compromise here and seek the middle course of a pragmatic conditional law between the morally right and the expedient. All politics must bend its knee before the right. But by this it can hope slowly to reach the stage where it will shine with an immortal glory.

APPENDIX II

OF THE HARMONY WHICH THE TRAN-SCENDENTAL CONCEPT OF PUBLIC RIGHT ESTABLISHES BETWEEN MORALITY AND POLITICS

If, like the teacher of law, I abstract from all the material of public law (i.e., abstract from the various empirically given relationships of men in the state or of states to each other), there remains only the *form* of publicity, the possibility of which is implied by every legal claim, since without it there can be no justice (which can only be conceived as publicly known) and thus no right, since it can be conferred only in accordance with justice. Every legal claim must be capable of publicity. Since it is easy to judge whether it is so in a particular case, i.e., whether it can be compatible with the principles of the agent, this gives an easily applied criterion found a priori in reason, by which the falsity (opposition to law) of the pretended claim (*praetensio iuris*) can, as it were, be immediately known by an experiment of pure reason.

Having set aside everything empirical in the concept of civil or international law (such as the wickedness in human nature which necessitates coercion), we can call the following proposition the transcendental formula of public law: "All actions relating to the right of other men are unjust if their maxim is not consistent with publicity."

This principle is to be regarded not merely as ethical (as belonging to the doctrine of virtue) but also as juridical (concerning the right of man). A maxim which I cannot divulge without defeating my own purpose must be kept secret if it is to succeed; and, if I cannot publicly avow it without inevitably exciting universal opposition to my project, the necessary and universal opposition which can be foreseen a priori is due only to the injustice with which the maxim threatens everyone. This principle is, furthermore, only negative, i.e., it only serves for the recognition of what is not just to others. Like an axiom, it is indemonstrably certain and, as will be seen in the following examples of public law, easily applied.

1. In the law of the state (*ius civitatis*) or domestic law, there is a question which many hold to be difficult to answer, yet it is easily solved by the transcendental principle of publicity. The question is: "Is rebellion a legitimate means for a people to employ in throwing off the yoke of an alleged tyrant (*non titulo, sed exercitio talis*)?" The rights of the people are injured; no injustice befalls the tyrant when he is deposed. There can be no doubt on this point. Nevertheless, it is in the highest degree illegitimate for the subjects to seek their rights in this way. If they fail in the struggle and are then subjected to severest punishment, they cannot complain about injustice any more than the tyrant could if they had succeeded.

If one wishes to decide this question by a dogmatic deduction of legal grounds, there can be much arguing pro and con; only the transcendental principle of the publicity of public law can free us of this prolixity. According to this principle, a people would ask itself before the establishment of the civil contract whether it dare publish the maxim of its intention to revolt on occasion. It is clear that if, in the establishment of a constitution, the condition is made that the people may in certain cases employ force against its chief, the people would have to pretend to a legitimate power over him, and then he would not be the chief. Or if both are made the condition of the establishment of the state, no state would be possible, though to establish it was the purpose of the people. The illegitimacy of rebellion is thus clear from the fact that its maxim, if openly acknowledged, would make its own purpose impossible. Therefore, it would have to be kept secret.

This secrecy, however, is not incumbent upon the chief of the state. He can openly say that he will punish every rebellion with the death of the ringleaders, however much they may believe that he was the first to overstep the basic law; for when he knows he possesses irresistible power (which must be assumed to be the case in every civil constitution, because he who does not have enough power to protect the people against every other also does not have the right to command them), he need not fear vitiating his own purpose by publishing his maxims. If the revolt of the people succeeds, what has been said is still quite compatible with the fact that the chief, on retiring to the status of a subject, cannot begin a revolt for his restoration but need not fear being made to account for his earlier administration of the state.

2. We can speak of international law only under the presupposition of some law-governed condition, i.e., of the external condition under which right can really be awarded to man. For, being a public law, it contains in its very concept the public announcement of a general will which assigns to each his rights, and this *status iuridicus* must result from some compact which is not founded on laws of compulsion (as in the case of the compact from which a single state arises). Rather, it must be founded on a free and enduring association, like the previously mentioned federation of states. For without there being some juridical condition, which actively binds together the different physical or moral persons, there can be only private law; this is the situation met with in the state of nature. Now here there is a conflict of politics with morality (regarding the latter as a science of right), and the criterion of publicity again finds an easy application in resolving it, though only if the compact between the states has been made with the purpose of preserving peace between them and other states, and not for conquest. The following cases of the antinomy between politics and morality occur (and they are stated with their solution).

a) "If one of these states has promised something to the other, such as aid, cession of some province, subsidies, and the like, and a case arises where the salvation of the state depends upon its being relieved of its promise, can it then consider itself in two roles: first as a sovereign (as it is responsible to no one in the state), and second as merely the highest official (who must give an account to the state)? From this dual capacity it would follow that in its latter role the state can relieve itself of what it has obliged itself to do in its former role." But if a state (or its chief) publicizes this maxim, others would naturally avoid entering an alliance with it, or ally themselves with others so as to resist such pretensions. This proves that politics with all its cunning would defeat its purpose by candor; therefore, that maxim must be illegitimate.

b) "If a neighboring power becomes formidable by its acquisitions (*potentia tremenda*), and thus causes anxiety, can one assume because it *can* oppress that it *will?* And does this give the lesser power, in union with others, a right to attack it without having first been injured by it?" A state which made known that such was its maxim would produce the feared evil even more certainly and quickly, for the greater power would steal a march on the smaller. And the alliance of the smaller powers would be only a feeble reed against one who knew how to apply the maxim *divide et impera*. This maxim of political expediency, if made public, would necessarily defeat its own purpose, and hence it is illegitimate.

c) "If a smaller state is so situated as to break up the territory of a larger one, and continuous territory is necessary to the preservation of the larger, is the latter not justified in subjugating the smaller and incorporating it?" We easily see that the greater power cannot afford to let this maxim become known; otherwise the smaller states would very early unite, or other powers would dispute the prey, and thus publicity would render this maxim impracticable. This is a sign that it is illegitimate. It may be unjust to a very high degree, for a small object of injustice does not prevent the injustice from being very great.

3. I say nothing about the law of world citizenship, for its analogy with international law makes it a very simple matter to state and evaluate its maxims.

Thus in the principle of incompatibility between the maxims of international law and publicity we have a good distinguishing mark for recognizing the nonconformity of politics to morality (as a science of right). Now we need to know the condition under which these maxims agree with the law of nations, for we cannot infer conversely that the maxims which bear publicity are therefore just, since no one who has decidedly superior power needs to conceal his plans. The condition of the possibility of international law in general is this: a juridical condition must first exist. For without this there is no public law, since all law which one may think of outside of this, in the state of nature, is merely private law. We have seen that a federation of states which has for its sole purpose the maintenance of peace is the only juridical condition compatible with the freedom of the several states. Therefore the harmony of politics with morals is possible only in a federative alliance, and the latter is necessary and given a priori by the principle of right. Furthermore, all politics has for its juridical basis the establishment of this harmony to its greatest possible extent, and without this end all its sophisms are but folly and veiled injustice. This false politics outdoes the best Jesuit school in casuistry. It has *reservatio mentalis*, wording public compacts with such expressions as can on occasion be interpreted to one's own advantage (for example, it makes the distinction between *status quo de fait* and *de droit*). It has *probabilism*, attributing hostile intentions to others, or even making probabilities of their possible superior power into legal grounds for destroying other, peaceful states. Finally, it has the *peccatum philosophicum* (*peccatillum, bagatelle*), holding it to be only a trifle when a small state is swallowed up in order that a much larger one may thereby approach more nearly to an alleged greater good for the world as a whole.[1]

The duplicity of politics in respect to morality, in using first one branch of it and then the other for its purposes, furthers these sophistic maxims. These branches are philanthropy and respect for the rights of men; and both are duty. The former is a conditional duty, while the latter is an unconditional and absolutely mandatory duty. One who wishes to give himself up to the sweet feeling of benevolence must make sure that he has not transgressed this absolute duty. Politics readily agrees with morality in its first branch (as ethics) in order to surrender the rights of men to their superiors. But with morality in the second branch (as a science of right), to which it must bend its knee, politics finds it advisable not to have any dealings, and rather denies it all reality, preferring to reduce all duties to mere benevolence. This artifice of a secretive politics would soon be unmasked by philosophy through publication of its maxims, if they only dared to allow the philosopher to publish his maxims.

In this regard I propose another affirmative and transcendental principle of public law, the formula of which is:

"All maxims which *stand in need* of publicity in order not to fail their end, agree with politics and right combined."

For if they can attain their end only through publicity, they must accord with the public's universal end, happi-

---

[1] The precedents for such maxims may be seen in Counselor Garve's treatise, *On the Union of Morality with Politics* (1788).* This worthy scholar admits in the beginning that he is not able to solve the problem completely. But to approve of this union while admitting that one cannot meet all objections which may be raised against it seems to show more tolerance than is advisable toward those who are inclined to abuse it.

* [Christian Garve (1742-98), *Abhandlung über die Verbindung der Moral mit der Politik oder einige Betrachtungen über die Frage, inwiefern es möglich sei, die Moral des Privatlebens bei der Regierung der Staaten zu beobachten* (Breslau, 1788).]

ness; and the proper task of politics is to promote this, i.e., to make the public satisfied with its condition. If, however, this end is attainable only by means of publicity, i.e., by removing all distrust in the maxims of politics, the latter must conform to the rights of the public, for only in this is the union of the goals of all possible.

The further development and discussion of this principle I must postpone to another occasion. But that it is a transcendental formula is to be seen from the exclusion of all empirical conditions (of the doctrine of happiness) as material of the law, and from the reference it makes to the form of universal lawfulness.

If it is a duty to make real (even if only through approximation in endless progress) the state of public law, and if there is well-grounded hope that this can actually be done, then perpetual peace, as the condition that will follow what has erroneously been called "treaties of peace" (but which in reality are only armistices), is not an empty idea. As the times required for equal steps of progress become, we hope, shorter and shorter, perpetual peace is a problem which, gradually working out its own solution, steadily approaches its goal.

ADDENDUM

SELECTION FROM THE *METAPHYSICS OF MORALS*

ADDENDUM

SELECTION FROM *THE METAPHYSICS OF MORALS*

[PERPETUAL PEACE AS A MORAL AND POLITICAL IDEAL] [1]

If one cannot prove that a certain thing is, he may try to prove that it is not. But if he does not succeed in either (as is often the case), he can still ask whether he is interested in assuming the one or the other by hypothesis. He may do this from either a theoretical or a practical point of view. That is, he may do so in order merely to explain a certain phenomenon (as the astronomer's phenomenon of the retrogression and station of the planets) or in order to reach a certain end. In the latter case, this end may be either pragmatic (an end of art) or moral, i.e., an end of such kind that the maxim to propose it is itself duty. It is self-evident that the assumption (*suppositio*) of the practicability of that end is not made a duty, as it is a merely theoretical and moreover a problematical judgment; for there is no obligation to believe anything. But action in accordance with the idea of that end, even when there is not the least theoretical probability that it can be realized, provided only that its impossibility cannot be demonstrated, is that to which a duty obligates us.

Now our moral-practical reason pronounces its irresistible veto: There ought not be war, neither that between me and thee in the state of nature nor that between us as states, which, though internally in a lawful condition, are externally, in relation to each other, in a lawless condition. For war is not the way in which each one should seek his

[1] [The selection is the conclusion of Part II of "Jurisprudence," and is titled simply "Conclusion."]

rights. Thus the question no longer is whether perpetual peace is something or nothing, and whether we delude ourselves in our theoretical judgment by assuming it to be something. Rather, we must act as if that thing, perpetual peace, existed—though it may not exist; we must endeavor to make it real and strive after the constitution (perhaps the republicanism of each and every state) which seems to us most likely to bring it to pass and to make an end to the disastrous warmaking to which all states without exception have directed their institutions as their chief end. And if the achievement of this purpose were to remain always only a pious wish, certainly in assuming a maxim of incessantly striving toward it we would at least not delude ourselves, for this is duty. But to assume that the moral law in us is deceptive would produce an abhorrent wish to dispense with all reason and to regard ourselves, by the nature of this wish, as subject to the same mechanism of nature as all other species of animals.

We can say that establishment of universal and enduring peace constitutes not just a part but rather the entire final end of jurisprudence within the limits of mere reason. Peace is the only condition under laws guaranteeing the mine and thine within a group of neighboring persons living together under a constitution whose rules are not derived from the experience of those who have fared best under it and whose experience, therefore, might serve as a norm for others. Rather, the rules must be derived by reason a priori from the ideal of a legal association of men under public laws generally, because all examples (which only illustrate and do not prove) are deceptive. Such rules, however, require a metaphysics, the necessity of which is carelessly conceded even by those who make fun of it.

This is seen, for example, when they say (as they often do), "The best constitution is one in which laws, not men, are sovereign." For what can be more metaphysically sublimated than this idea which, according to their own assertion, has the most assured objective reality, and which is readily borne out by actual events? And this idea alone, if it is not taken in a revolutionary sense and made the basis of sudden change through violent overthrow of a previously existing wrong condition—this idea alone, I say, if it is sought for and realized by gradual reform in the light of firm principles, can uninterruptedly lead to the highest political good, perpetual peace.

The Library of Liberal Arts